101
MASTERPIECES
of
AMERICAN PRIMITIVE PAINTING

101
MASTERPIECES
of
AMERICAN PRIMITIVE PAINTING

from the Collection of
EDGAR WILLIAM & BERNICE CHRYSLER GARBISCH

FOREWORD BY
JAMES J. RORIMER
Director, The Metropolitan Museum of Art

PREFACE BY
JOHN WALKER
Director, National Gallery of Art

INTRODUCTION BY
ALBERT TEN EYCK GARDNER
Associate Curator of American Painting and Sculpture
The Metropolitan Museum of Art

NEW EDITION

PUBLISHED BY
THE AMERICAN FEDERATION OF ARTS

DISTRIBUTED BY
DOUBLEDAY & COMPANY, INC.

FIRST EDITION 1961

NEW EDITION 1962

EXHIBITION SCHEDULE

IOI MASTERPIECES OF AMERICAN PRIMITIVE PAINTING
from the Collection of
EDGAR WILLIAM & BERNICE CHRYSLER GARBISCH
IN THE UNITED STATES OF AMERICA
UNDER THE AUSPICES OF
THE AMERICAN FEDERATION OF ARTS
[1961–1964]

1961–62

November 17–January 7	The Metropolitan Museum of Art, New York, New York

1962

February 10–March 11	Walker Art Center, Minneapolis, Minnesota
March 30–April 30	Columbus Gallery of Fine Arts, Columbus, Ohio
May 15–June 17	City Art Museum of St. Louis, St. Louis, Missouri
June 28–July 30	Municipal Art Gallery, Los Angeles, California
August 15–September 15	M. H. de Young Memorial Museum, San Francisco, California
October 14–November 14	Atlanta Art Association Galleries, Atlanta, Georgia
December 7–30	Virginia Museum of Fine Arts, Richmond, Virginia

1963

January 15–February 12	Cincinnati Art Museum, Cincinnati, Ohio
February 28–March 31	The Art Institute of Chicago, Chicago, Illinois

April 16–May 15	Carnegie Institute, Pittsburgh, Pennsylvania
May 30–June 30	Amon Carter Museum of Western Art, Fort Worth, Texas
July 15–August 15	Rochester Memorial Art Gallery, Rochester, New York
September 5–30	Milwaukee Art Center, Milwaukee, Wisconsin
October 15–November 17	Isaac Delgado Museum of Art, New Orleans, Louisiana
December 1–30	Baltimore Museum of Art, Baltimore, Maryland

1964

January 15–February 15	Philadelphia Museum of Art, Philadelphia, Pennsylvania
March 5–29	Museum of Fine Arts, Boston, Massachusetts
April 14–May 15	Detroit Institute of Arts, Detroit, Michigan

*(The opening and closing dates listed for the
exhibition periods are in some cases approximate)*

*The American Federation of Arts, with headquarters at 41 East 65th Street,
New York City, is a national non-profit, educational organization, founded 1909
in Washington, D. C. and incorporated 1916 in the State of New York. It is
composed of chapter, individual, and corporate members. The purpose of the
Federation is to cultivate the appreciation and foster the production of art in
America. This is carried out through a program of activities including traveling
exhibitions, publications, national and regional conferences
and consultation services.*

FOREWORD

WEBSTER's definition of the word "primitive" includes the following words: "Characterized by the manner, style, simplicity, rudeness, or the like, of a former time; old-fashioned."

Since the time of the earliest cavemen, or thereabouts, men—and often women— have wanted to express visually their feelings, their reactions, their beliefs, on walls, on ceilings, on a piece of zinc or paper or on a piece of furniture. The expression of emotions, sentiments, and deep, perhaps unconscious, urges has produced paintings that are as different as Michelangelo's work in the Sistine Chapel and the prepared canvas scattered with drops of paint or even brushed with a single color.

From colonial times well into the nineteenth century some of our American fore- bears expressed themselves with renderings of fruits and flowers, birds and beasts, pictures of their surroundings and of their dear ones. The galaxy of the *101 Master- pieces of American Primitive Painting* from the collection of Edgar William and Bernice Chrysler Garbisch tells of the sincerity and fortitude of the early settlers and the artists who painted them. These were not courtiers from the pleasure-seeking coterie surrounding the kings of France, nor Roman warriors, nor Egyptian slaves; these were God-fearing, self-respecting pioneer Americans who found hard work and rewards for their work in a slowly developing society. Some, both patrons and painters, had close ties with their lands of origin. The English country squire or early academician from London often influenced those who saw his pictures or had expe- riences similar to his. The shipment to America of works of art, whether English or French, often gave inspiration to American painters. On the other hand a Benjamin West renounced the ways of his early style when he took up residence in England.

There is no reason to be condescending or diffident about the American primitive and its place in the history of art. A Byzantine mosaic or a Spanish fresco cannot be judged solely in the terms of Raphael's *Disputà* or a Roger van der Weyden portrait or religious painting any more than a photograph should be judged by the standards of a nineteenth-century French academician or Impressionist painter. How can we gainsay giving a place in our museums to these direct, often accomplished, performances of the "primitive" artist?

To evaluate art in its many ramifications, we must accept a vocabulary which is all-inclusive, not just the "lingo" of the romantic, the prosaic, the advanced or the sophisticated artists and thinkers of one generation or another. Each philosophy has its limitations and in terms of another may become outmoded. The universal mind has achieved sentiments and expressions of lasting, or at least recurring, impetus. In our day we may accept many of the precepts of the Greek philosopher and may find the medieval mind limited by unacceptable convictions. Both rational and irrational observations may be fashionable in one place or at one period and most unacceptable at others.

Returning to the present-day use of the word "primitive," we must examine the entire gamut of all our civilizations. The works of art from pre-historic cultures are no longer considered inept and barbarous because we have found for ourselves that a Cycladic marble has a message not to be discovered in a fifth-century Attic sculpture, an Italian primitive, or a Gothic painting. Perhaps a Byzantine Madonna, a Cimabue or a Duccio *Maestà* does not meet the requirements of a Murillo or a Rubens, but the message may be as real and even as poignant when it is understood.

There have been a few collectors in the American primitive field who by familiarity and intensive study and selection have been awakened and are awakening others to the virtues and respectability of their particular collecting passions. It is a remarkable commentary on collecting in our own times that Colonel and Mrs. Garbisch have chosen to live with eighteenth-century French furniture and French Impressionist and post-Impressionist paintings in their New York home, and seventeenth- and eighteenth-century American furniture and American primitives in their beautiful Maryland manor house.

In a great encyclopedic museum like the Metropolitan we show *September Morn* by a forgotten artist, a Pollock which is among the masters of the current rage, along with our Grecos, Rembrandts and Master of Flémalle and Georges de La Tour. American primitives were stimulating and attractive in their time, and their day has again come back. An unknown, unrecorded Pennsylvania or Massachusetts portrait painter today shares the limelight of wider focus. Our terms of reference today are universal, encyclopedic, not limited in their scope nor shrouded in misconceptions of terminology and contrived platitudes.

James J. Rorimer, *Director*
THE METROPOLITAN MUSEUM OF ART
New York, New York

PREFACE

EVERYONE interested in art owes a debt to Edgar William and Bernice Chrysler Garbisch. They have assembled the most extensive and important collection of American primitive paintings ever brought together. This in itself is a remarkable achievement. But of still greater significance, they have rescued numerous canvases and panels that were rapidly deteriorating and would soon have vanished completely.

Collecting is often an arduous pursuit. Ever since their first purchases of American primitive paintings, Colonel and Mrs. Garbisch have devoted a large part of their time to a search for the finest examples, to a study of those already collected, and to the investigation of problems in restoration and preservation. Since their original gift of a part of their collection was made to the National Gallery of Art in 1953, I have been privileged to watch them at work, and I know something of their excitement during their quest for new pictures; their anxiety while a panel or canvas, obscured by dirt and almost impenetrable varnish, is being cleaned in accordance with their strict standards of restoration; the effort they put into research, into the pursuit of a correct attribution, if not to a known artist at least to the anonymous painter of a similar group of works; and finally the pains they take in framing their paintings, either restoring the original frames or finding other American frames of the kind the artists themselves might have chosen.

An important result of such concentrated attention to a particular field of collecting is that Colonel and Mrs. Garbisch are now acknowledged to be the outstanding collectors of American primitive paintings and are, therefore, almost invariably given the first choice by dealers and private owners. This does not diminish their own initiative; they still look for hidden and forgotten masterpieces. At the same time, their success as collectors has brought with it a corresponding disadvantage. Many other collectors have followed in their footsteps; and as demand has exceeded supply, the competition for American primitive paintings of excellent quality has become

American Primitive Painting

very keen. I am sure the reaction of Colonel and Mrs. Garbisch to this new appreciation of our American primitives is mixed. Although enlarging their collection has become more difficult for them, still this rise in value means that more of the precious examples of the work of American primitive limners that have been deteriorating for years, forgotten in attics and barns, are being rediscovered and preserved.

After all, to stimulate an enjoyment and appreciation of American primitive painting has been the real goal of Colonel and Mrs. Garbisch. I concur in their belief that our primitives have a particular significance. They mirror vividly the life, the customs, and the general appearance of our ancestors and of the world in which they lived. American primitive paintings are beautiful in themselves, inventive in their linear patterns, decorative in their pure and simple colors, and effective in their analysis of human character and in their revelation of unusual aspects of the beauty of nature. Moreover, they are destined, I believe, to become an inspiration to future painters. For there are indications that the contribution of non-objective art is diminishing and that painters are gradually returning to representation. Their emergence from abstraction is not in the direction of academic painting. They are seeking to see the world with a fresh and innocent eye, and freshness of vision is a particular quality of our primitive painters. Thus American primitive painting may well provide a guide which future artists will cherish and follow.

The present exhibition, a very small part of the immense collection formed by Colonel and Mrs. Garbisch, offers an opportunity to evaluate the work of our primitive artists. Modest craftsmen, unself-conscious in their work, they pretended to no exalted position. From their honesty and integrity resulted an original, truly American style, a style beautifully revealed in the *101 Masterpieces of American Primitive Painting* which will now tour the United States.

John Walker, *Director*
NATIONAL GALLERY OF ART
Washington, D. C.

TABLE OF CONTENTS

Paintings lent by the National Gallery of Art from those given by Edgar William and Bernice Chrysler Garbisch from their collection of American primitive paintings.

INTRODUCTION

THE collection of American primitive paintings which Edgar William and Bernice Chrysler Garbisch have brought together over a period of more than seventeen years is the most comprehensive of its kind yet assembled; although no final count is ever possible, since the collection grows all the while, it now consists of almost two thousand five hundred pictures. In 1953 Colonel and Mrs. Garbisch gave a selection of paintings from their collection to the National Gallery of Art in Washington, D. C. Now, in view of the growth of the collection, they are contemplating the eventual distribution of selected groups to other important museums throughout the United States. In the meantime those paintings not yet given are kept in various places; usually the newest acquisitions are to be found in the Colonel's office in New York City. Certain favorite pictures ornament the rooms of a charming manor house on the Eastern Shore of Maryland. In fact it was the decoration of this country home that started Colonel and Mrs. Garbisch on their enthusiastic search for these colorful mementos of the American past.

But with the constant expansion of the collection, this original project has grown into the management of a vast private museum of American pictures, with all the attendant problems of storage and display, of framing, cataloging, restoration. But these serious museum problems are outweighed by the collectors' search for new treasures and by the thrill of discovering new masterpieces.

The amazingly successful search for these enchanting, or hilarious, or forbidding examples of our native art is due entirely to the boundless enthusiasm of Colonel and Mrs. Garbisch. It is through the enthusiasm of such dedicated collectors, who have often saved these paintings from destruction, that we are now able to enjoy so many American primitive paintings in all their unsophisticated glory. Some of them are undoubtedly jolly masterpieces of rustic humor, yet others are shy and tender statements of quaint formality. To some minds these paintings are most interesting as proof of the universal urge to paint, to draw, to ornament, to enliven and enhance, to glorify the plain or rough surfaces of life with pictures, with colors, with rhythmic patterns of joyful exuberance.

Those who fall under the spell of American primitive paintings are on occasion forced to defend the sometimes highly specialized charms of these pictures, warding off the attacks of those who are not familiar with American history; of those who do not know the basic precepts of painting; of those who lack any trace of that special feeling of romantic nostalgia for the rusticities of yesteryear. Such unfortunate people are not properly prepared to consider American primitive paintings with the seriousness and delight they deserve.

Colonel and Mrs. Garbisch published in the magazine *Art in America* a brief statement about American primitive paintings, saying, "They merit an important place not only in the history of American art but in the history of world art as well." And indeed it is now necessary to consider American primitive paintings from just such a broad point of view.

The appreciation of primitive art and folk art has been termed "the appreciation of the art of the unself-conscious by the self-conscious." It is a phenomenon that appears only in highly sophisticated societies. Folk art, peasant art, and primitive art at their own true levels are valued by maker and user for their ritualistic or ornamental use; these things were made for special purposes, and the fulfillment of these purposes is what the true primitive, the folk, and the peasant demand.

In these paintings we see the unfettered hand of the "primitive" painter—amateur or artisan—dashing forward into difficult artistic problems with sublime self-confidence. These problems are attacked with a free-wheeling abandon unhindered by the laws of perspective or gravity, unawed by the grand pronouncements of the official European academies of art, by the time-honored precepts of the old masters of Renaissance Europe, or by the sacred writings of ancient Greek or Roman critics of painting. The freedom of the frontier, the almost total isolation of many rural communities, encouraged the amateur artists to go ahead on their own. Thus the American primitive paintings reflect the spirit of their time. They preserve with a wholesome simplicity the natural visions of the painter whose eye and hand were neither guided nor corrupted by the artistic theories of the Renaissance.

In these paintings is summed up a number of important aspects of the spirit of the American people. Although there are unsophisticated crudities here and there, and naïvetés in plenty, yet above and beyond all these faults—if they are faults—is the good-humored expression of self-confidence, or of a desire for medieval color and ornamentation, rather than for the more subtle Renaissance, Leonardesque beauties of sophisticated academic painting.

In the art of the American primitive painter one finds two great qualities—humor and candor—that are usually concealed, if not entirely lacking, in the more formal, more sophisticated and self-conscious forms of European and American academic painting of the time. A rollicking sense of humor is revealed in many primitive genre paintings; and in his primitive portraits the artist has observed his subjects with a hard-eyed and unsparing candor piercing beyond mere pattern or caricature, or anatomy, into regions of psychological depth which no academically trained "society" portrait painter has ever dared to explore. But humor and candor were typical early American characteristics—the humor of the American frontier is broad and Chaucerian; the uncompromising candor is perhaps a result of frontier democracy.

Many American primitive paintings are the works of amateurs who painted for the sheer pleasure of painting; the work itself was its own reward. But in all these pictures one finds medieval displays of humor and free invention—there is a simplicity, a directness, a liveliness that one automatically associates with American freedom. Perhaps no small part of their appeal to a neurotic and sophisticated age is that in them we see the primitive artist courageously plunging into strange realms to find the means with which to express his solid convictions about the world as he knew it; he has preserved for us nostalgic images and scenes of innocence and tranquility.

According to Colonel and Mrs. Garbisch, "to really understand American primitive painting, one must have at least a basic knowledge of American history, for that is the only way one can get a true concept of the people whose spirit and character these paintings so vividly reflect."

Though the facts of the political, military, and economic history of the American Revolution are well known, one of the most significant results of that history was the change in the status of persons; the transformation of provincial colonists into independent Americans. After the Revolution the vast landholdings of many Tory families were broken up and sold in small lots. Any man could take his axe and hoe and set out into the wilderness and start a farm for himself, clearing the land and building his own house.

The man who could plan and put up even a simple log house—though he might never build a Parthenon—must possess in some degree the three-dimensional imagination of the artist, the architect, the engineer; and, having this all-important faculty, he would be able to solve the problems in making the design for a building, for an engineering project, for a machine, or for the painting of a picture.

Although there were more artisans and amateur painters at work in provincial America in the seventeenth and eighteenth centuries than is generally supposed, the great burgeoning of American primitive art did not occur until after the American Revolution, and it came to its fullest development in the first half of the nineteenth century. The cause of this is interesting to speculate upon.

Perhaps the new-found freedom and independence, of which every American was then so conscious, encouraged an experimental adventurousness in the minds of many artisans and craftsmen, who turned their hands to painting pictures when they found themselves released from restrictions imposed on them by custom or by British parliamentarians. Then, too, the new nation was an attractive haven for the many skilled craftsmen from England and the Continent—men who were eager to escape from the fixed social caste system in Europe which restricted their movements, their ownership of property, their independence, their chance for advancement.

It was a society dominated by rural individualists (as most of America was in the first half of the nineteenth century), men and women whose practical, down-to-earth views and reliance on empirical experience led them to advance by experiment and observation rather than by scientific theories. In such a society the amateur or primitive painter found an atmosphere that encouraged him to experiment as a self-taught painter and to record the observations of his own eyes. Thus, his paintings developed in an American vein and had a firm local character.

Few of the American colonists came from large urban centers in Europe where they might have had contact with Renaissance ideas about painting. Though these ideas were current among the aristocracy, the yeomen and farmers and middle-class merchants and craftsmen knew little of such things. Most colonists were intent on building a new way of life for themselves and their children, and in colonial America they had little time for the fripperies of courtiers or the savants.

As the first colonists in New England brought with them medieval traditions of house building, so they unconsciously carried to the New World medieval traditions of painting and decorating.

The use of the term "medieval" does not imply that the American primitive painters were in any sense *trained* painters of any of the medieval European schools of painting; but rather that they worked naturally in the old medieval manner rather than in the self-conscious Italian Renaissance academic manner. They were not concerned with the inexorable mathematics of Alberti's laws of perspective, they had no rules for *chiaroscuro*, they had no knowledge of anatomy. Their vision was not formed upon the classic Mediterranean shapes of ancient Greece and Rome. They were in fact almost completely untouched by the Italian Renaissance disciplines.

Lacking academic paraphernalia, the American primitive artist fell into the mode of medieval painting of northern Europe where symbolic shapes and bright colors represented what the painter knew and felt rather than what he saw. Thus the gaudy colors, the hieratic poses, the non-Greco-Roman compositions of American primitive painting are related to the styles of painting to be seen in early illuminated manuscripts and in the wall paintings of medieval times. Curiously close parallels can be found between the two types of painting. In many portraits by American primitive painters are to be found the same sort of short-hand symbols for eyes, noses, mouths, and hands that one finds in medieval manuscript illuminations or in Spanish romanesque mural paintings.

The very great number of American primitive portraits is partly explained when we remember that before the invention of the camera the painted portrait had the function of marking the various stages of social life and the rituals of living and dying. Thus, there were many portraits of infants and children; many pairs of wedding portraits; many memorial portraits of the dead. This traditional attitude toward portraits is but another link between the medieval European painting tradition and that of the American primitive.

There are curiously interesting differences between the paintings produced in America in the seventeenth and eighteenth centuries and those produced in the nineteenth century. The differences stem from the attitudes of the artists toward their work and from the kind of patronage offered to them in the two eras. Primitive pictures of the seventeenth and eighteenth centuries were for the most part sturdy and ambitious provincial attempts to produce approximations to current European styles of painting—usually in more or less formal portraits. The provincial artist learned of these styles from engravings and mezzotints imported from Europe.

Most primitive painters and limners were engaged in trades that were in some way related to the arts. They were house painters, sign painters, silversmiths, or engravers. But some were aspiring young men who wanted to conquer the grand art world of London, as Benjamin West, Matthew Pratt, Ralph Earle, and John Singleton Copley did. But most of the American primitive painters of the nineteenth century were more modest and local in their ambitions. They were satisfied to be Americans and to embellish their daily lives in Seneca Falls; Paris, Maine; or Shickshinny, Pennsylvania. This they did with rustic painted records of their time; with precisely tinted dreams of unknown grandeur, or with devastating direct statements in paint about their contemporaries, in the form of portraits.

In the eighteenth and nineteenth centuries, when so many Americans turned their hands to painting, they were close to the traditional home handicrafts and household industries. In the old days every man had many highly developed manual skills, and if he did not know how to handle a woodsman's axe he could manage the whittler's knife. And every housewife knew the arts of spinning, weaving, sewing, dyeing, and a thousand other handicrafts and skills—candles and soap and coats and breeches were all made at home. Thus, there was a vast population in America with diversified manual skills. Woodsman, farmer, urban craftsman, and homeowner knew how to build whatever they might need, and their wives were artists who could produce good loaves of bread as well as handsome bits of embroidery and weaving.

The many hands thus trained in the exercise of many skills found it easy to take up the brush and dash off a landscape, a portrait, or a fanciful composition.

When the industries and crafts were separated from the home, the pursuit of the handicrafts suffered a severe setback. When the sign painter's family no longer lived in the shop and assisted in the tasks at hand, when the loom and spinning wheel became mechanized monsters and moved out of the home, everyone suffered. There was, of course, less drudgery, but this improvement was offset by the loss of opportunity to develop at home the instinctive skills of the craftsman which had been handed down from father to son, from mother to daughter, since medieval times.

Today, when the do-it-yourself fashion is forcing many apartment dwellers on the New Frontier to learn the antique virtues of self-sufficiency, we can appreciate the skills of our ancestors who could so handily turn out a pair of boots, a length of cloth, a seaworthy sloop, or a painting.

The serious nature of the loss of household arts and skills—through lack of opportunity to develop them in the old-fashioned way—was recognized later in the nineteenth century. Lessons in drawing and design were introduced into the public schools in Philadelphia and Boston, and "industrial art" schools were established. A school of design for women was instituted in Philadelphia as early as 1844, and in the next decade The Cooper Union in New York was offering courses in drawing and painting for women.

Modern enthusiasm for American primitive paintings is found among several distinct groups whose interests do not usually run in parallel. These groups are the antiquarians and collectors of American antiques—the first to collect such pictures in the late nineteenth century—and the modern artists and collectors of modern art, who recognized in these paintings the same naïve, unacademic charms found in the arts of truly primitive tribes of Asia, Africa, and America. Another group that sees a special value in American primitive paintings is the social historians, who find in them a fascinating record of the culture and social structure of other days.

These pictures do preserve a fascinating American record of places and faces; of fashions and manners; enough to engage the rapt attention of the scholarly sociologist and the historian as well as the eye of the modern painters, professional and amateur; for modern painters can study these free and often daring experiments in design and color with real profit.

American primitive paintings can no longer be considered merely as charming antiques. We look at them now without the condescension of the academic artist, without the limiting, local specializations of the antique collector, without the special, somewhat patronizing attitudes of the lover of modern art. We see these pictures in their true perspective as an important part of American art history and in their correct relation to the history of the art of the Western World.

In one of the first books on painting published in English there is a remarkable description of the special qualities we find in American primitive painting—in the art of the amateur as well as in the work of the trained but unsophisticated craftsman. In *The Painting of the Ancients* by Franciscus Junius, published in 1638, we read:

> The painter . . . playeth youthfully . . . which signifieth, to doe a thing with such courage, pleasantnesse, and ease, that the work may be perceived to proceed out of a lusty and vigorous youthfulnesse; and certainly, the chiefest and most lively force of Art consisteth herein, that there appears in the work that same prosperously prompt and fertile Facilitie which useth to accompany our first endeavours; that is the very life and spirit of art; which if it be extinguished with too much care of trimming, the whole work will be but a dead and lifelesse thing.

> . . . pictures surpassing the apprehension and art of Man . . . insinuate nothing els but that there is something in them which doth not proceed from laborious curiositie prescribed by the rules of art, and that the free spirit of the artificer marking how Nature sporteth herselfe in such an infinite variety of things, undertooke to do the same.

Albert Ten Eyck Gardner
*Associate Curator of
American Painting and Sculpture*
THE METROPOLITAN MUSEUM OF ART
New York, New York

101
MASTERPIECES
of
AMERICAN PRIMITIVE PAINTING

Jonathan Benham BY AN UNKNOWN ARTIST, ABOUT 1710

PLATE I

Gentleman of the Ten Eyck Family BY AN UNKNOWN ARTIST, ABOUT 1710

PLATE 2

Lady of the Ten Eyck Family BY AN UNKNOWN ARTIST, ABOUT 1710

PLATE 3

The Annunciation BY AN UNKNOWN ARTIST, ABOUT 1710

PLATE 4

"Christ Talketh with a Woman of Samaria" BY AN UNKNOWN ARTIST, ABOUT 1710

PLATE 5

Catalynje Post BY AN UNKNOWN ARTIST, ABOUT 1730

PLATE 6

Susanna Truax BY AN UNKNOWN ARTIST, 1730

PLATE 7

Lady with Beaded Headdress BY AN UNKNOWN ARTIST, ABOUT 1730

PLATE 8

Young Lady with a Rose ATTRIBUTED TO PIETER VANDERLYN, 1732

PLATE 9

Margaret Robins BY JOHN HESSELIUS, ABOUT 1745

PLATE 10

Young Lady with a Fan BY AN UNKNOWN ARTIST, 1737

PLATE II

Mrs. Isaac Foster BY JOSEPH BADGER, 1755

PLATE 12

Devout Lady ATTRIBUTED TO JEREMIAH THEUS, ABOUT 1750

PLATE 13

Sarah Whitehead Hubbard by John Durand, 1768

PLATE 14

Sarah Ursula Rose BY BENJAMIN WEST, 1756

PLATE 15

Mary Boticon Lathrop by John Durand, about 1770

PLATE 16

Catharine Hendrickson BY AN UNKNOWN ARTIST, 1770

PLATE 17

The Domino Girl BY AN UNKNOWN ARTIST, ABOUT 1775

PLATE 18

Miss Denison BY AN UNKNOWN ARTIST, ABOUT 1785

PLATE 19

Captain Samuel Chandler BY WINTHROP CHANDLER, ABOUT 1780

PLATE 20

Mrs. Samuel Chandler BY WINTHROP CHANDLER, ABOUT 1780

PLATE 21

The Start of the Hunt BY AN UNKNOWN ARTIST, ABOUT 1780

PLATE 22

The End of the Hunt BY AN UNKNOWN ARTIST, ABOUT 1780

PLATE 23

Job Perit BY REUBEN MOULTHROP, 1790

PLATE 24

Sally Perit BY REUBEN MOULTHROP, 1790

PLATE 25

The American Star by Frederick Kemmelmeyer, about 1795

PLATE 26

Lady with Her Pets (Molly Whales Leonard) BY RUFUS HATHAWAY, 1790

PLATE 27

Emma Van Name BY AN UNKNOWN ARTIST, ABOUT 1795

PLATE 28

Washington Reviewing the Western Army at Fort Cumberland, Maryland
BY FREDERICK KEMMELMEYER, ABOUT 1795

PLATE 29

The Home of George Washington, "The Father of His Country" BY J. WIESS, 1797

PLATE 30

Mrs. Noah Smith and Her Children by RALPH EARL, 1798

PLATE 31

Family Portrait BY RALPH E. W. EARL, 1804

PLATE 32

The Sargent Family BY AN UNKNOWN ARTIST, 1800

PLATE 33

Edward and Sarah Rutter BY JOSHUA JOHNSTON, ABOUT 1805

PLATE 34

In the Garden ATTRIBUTED TO JOSHUA JOHNSTON, ABOUT 1805

PLATE 35

The Battle of New Orleans BY HYACINTHE DE LACLOTTE, 1815

PLATE 36

A Ceremonial at a Young Ladies' Seminary BY AN UNKNOWN ARTIST, ABOUT 1810

PLATE 37

Alice Slade by Ammi Phillips, 1816

PLATE 38

Joseph Slade BY AMMI PHILLIPS, 1816

PLATE 39

Mr. Tiffen of East Kingston, New Hampshire ATTRIBUTED TO A. ELLIS, ABOUT 1820

PLATE 40

Oneida Chieftain Shikellamy BY AN UNKNOWN ARTIST, ABOUT 1820

PLATE 41

Horizon of the New World BY AN UNKNOWN ARTIST, ABOUT 1825

PLATE 42

Bowl of Fruit BY AN UNKNOWN ARTIST, ABOUT 1830

PLATE 43

Market Square, Germantown, Pennsylvania BY WILLIAM BRITTON, ABOUT 1820

PLATE 44

U. S. Revenue Cutter BY H. A. ROATH, ABOUT 1825

PLATE 45

The Plantation BY AN UNKNOWN ARTIST, ABOUT 1825

PLATE 46

This great o'erwhelming work of awful Time
In all its dread magnificence sublime,

Above, below, where'er the astonished eye
Turns to behold, new opening wonders lie,

Rises on our view, amid a crashing roar
That bids us kneel, and Time's great God adore.

With uproar hideous first the *Falls* appear,
The stunning tumult thundering on the ear.

of Niagara

25

The Falls

18

The Falls of Niagara by Edward Hicks, 1825

PLATE 47

General Washington on White Charger (Jack) BY AN UNKNOWN ARTIST, ABOUT 1830

PLATE 48

Mary Werner Bangs by ERASTUS SALISBURY FIELD, ABOUT 1830

PLATE 49

Mrs. John Harrison and Her Daughter Maria by Nathaniel Mayhew, 1823

PLATE 50

Sea Captain Maxwell B. Chace BY AN UNKNOWN ARTIST, ABOUT 1835

PLATE 51

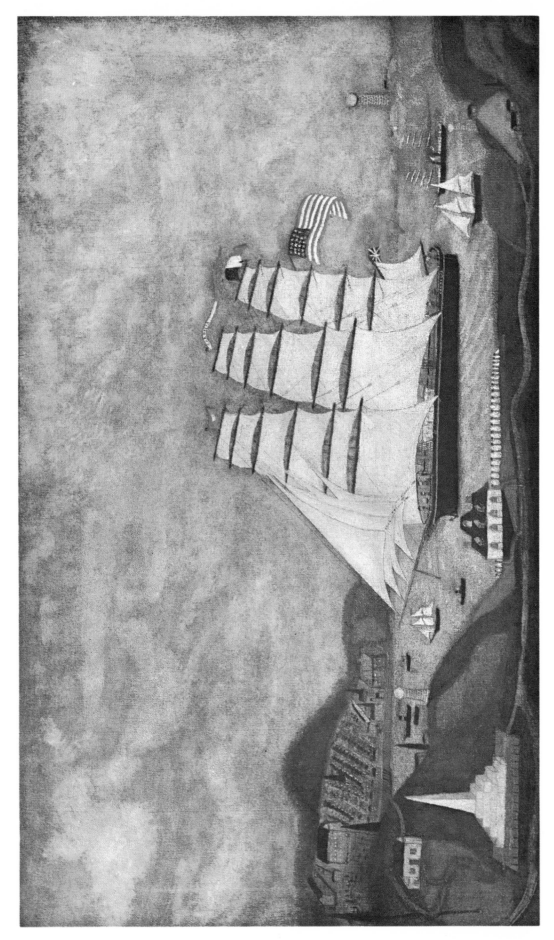

Yankee Clipper "Cardelia" BY AN UNKNOWN ARTIST, ABOUT 1830

PLATE 52

Peaceable Kingdom BY EDWARD HICKS, ABOUT 1830

PLATE 53

Basket of Fruit with Flowers BY AN UNKNOWN ARTIST, ABOUT 1830

PLATE 54

GLORY TO GOD ON HIGH.

The Adoration of the Shepherds and the Magi BY AN UNKNOWN ARTIST, ABOUT 1830

PLATE 55

Fruit and Flowers BY AN UNKNOWN ARTIST, ABOUT 1835

PLATE 56

The Family at Home BY H. KNIGHT, 1836

PLATE 57

Baby in Wicker Basket by JOSEPH WHITING STOCK, ABOUT 1840

PLATE 58

Mrs. Mayer and Daughter ATTRIBUTED TO AMMI PHILLIPS, ABOUT 1835

PLATE 59

Blue Eyes BY AN UNKNOWN ARTIST, ABOUT 1840

PLATE 60

Agnes Frazee and Child BY AN UNKNOWN ARTIST, 1834

PLATE 61

On Point BY D. G. STOUTER, ABOUT 1840

PLATE 62

The Cat BY AN UNKNOWN ARTIST, ABOUT 1840

PLATE 63

In Full Stride BY AN UNKNOWN ARTIST, ABOUT 1840

PLATE 64

Dismal Swamp BY GEORGE WASHINGTON MARK, 1840

PLATE 65

The Hobby Horse BY AN UNKNOWN ARTIST, ABOUT 1840

PLATE 66

Vermont Lawyer by Horace Bundy, 1841

PLATE 67

Portrait of a Man BY AN UNKNOWN ARTIST, ABOUT 1840

PLATE 68

Portrait of a Woman BY AN UNKNOWN ARTIST, ABOUT 1840

PLATE 69

Tea Time BY AN UNKNOWN ARTIST, ABOUT 1840

PLATE 70

Man of Science BY M. KRANZ [?], 1839

PLATE 71

Little Girl in Lavender BY JOHN BRADLEY, ABOUT 1840

PLATE 72

The Constitution and Guerrière BY THOMAS CHAMBERS, ABOUT 1845

PLATE 73

Indian Lament BY AN UNKNOWN ARTIST, ABOUT 1850

PLATE 74

The Cornell Farm BY EDWARD HICKS, 1848

PLATE 75

A City of Fantasy BY AN UNKNOWN ARTIST, ABOUT 1850

PLATE 76

"He Turned Their Waters into Blood" BY ERASTUS SALISBURY FIELD, ABOUT 1845

PLATE 77

"He That Tilleth His Land Shall Be Satisfied" BY AN UNKNOWN ARTIST, ABOUT 1850

PLATE 78

Hudson River Valley, Sunset by Thomas Chambers, about 1850

PLATE 79

Peaceful Village BY AN UNKNOWN ARTIST, ABOUT 1850

PLATE 80

Stylized Landscape BY AN UNKNOWN ARTIST, ABOUT 1850

PLATE 81

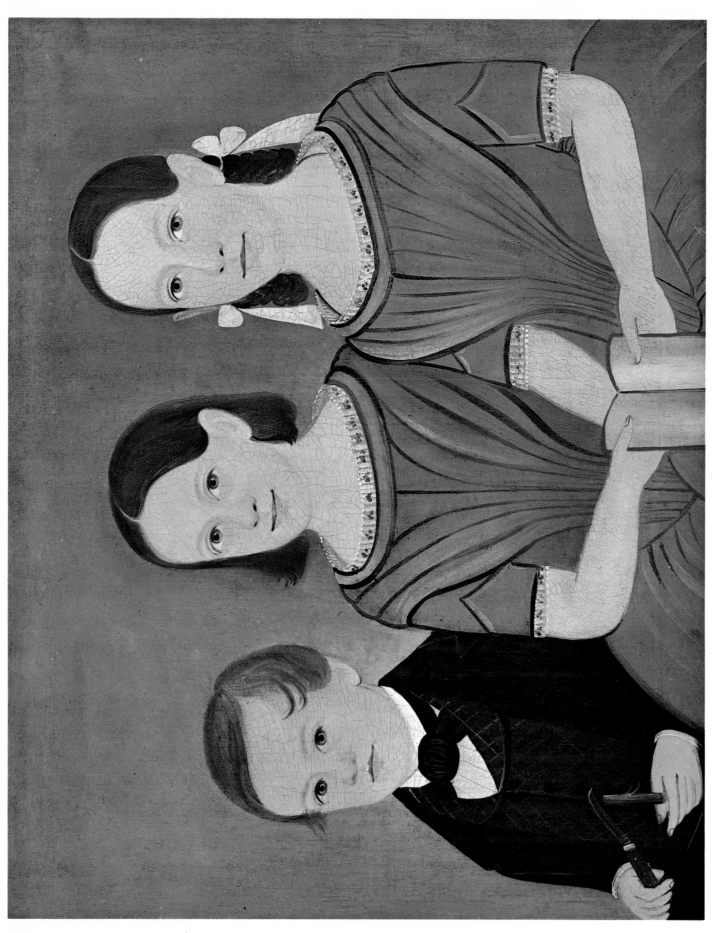

The Younger Generation ATTRIBUTED TO WILLIAM MATTHEW PRIOR, ABOUT 1850

PLATE 82

By the Cool and Shady Rill BY AN UNKNOWN ARTIST, ABOUT 1850

PLATE 83

Reception of General Louis Kossuth at New York City, December 24, 1850,
BY E. PERCEL, ABOUT 1850

PLATE 84

The Tow Boat Conqueror BY JAMES I. EVANS, 1852

PLATE 85

Memorial to Nicholas M. S. Catlin BY SUSANE WALTERS, 1852

PLATE 86

The Burnish Sisters by William Matthew Prior, 1854

PLATE 87

The Neigh of an Iron Horse BY A. TAPY, 1859

PLATE 88

Studebaker in His Wagon-Tire Shop, Hangtown, California BY H. M. T. POWELL, ABOUT 1855

PLATE 89

Flax Scutching Bee by LINTON PARK, ABOUT 1860

PLATE 90

Bare Knuckles by George A. Hayes, about 1860

PLATE 91

Poestenkill, New York by Joseph H. Hidley, about 1855

PLATE 92

Mahantango Valley Farm BY AN UNKNOWN ARTIST, ABOUT 1860

PLATE 93

Fruit of the Seasons BY KOST, ABOUT 1860

PLATE 94

Confederate Blockade Runner and Union Man-of-War BY F. R. MULLEN, 1861

PLATE 95

Custer's Last Fight, June 25, 1876 BY W. J. WALLACK, 1876

PLATE 96

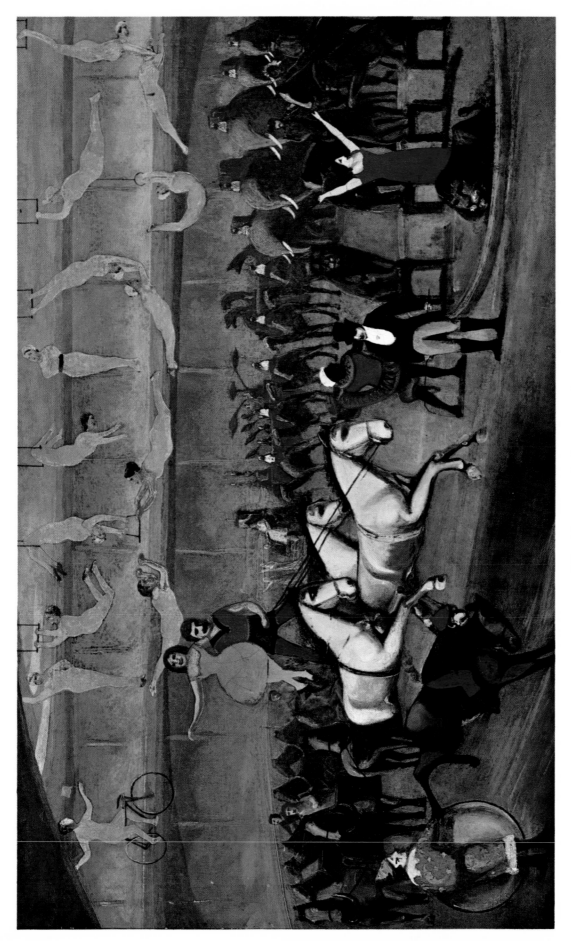

The Circus BY A. LOGAN, 1874

PLATE 97

Chilly Observation BY CHARLES S. RALEIGH, 1889

PLATE 98

Berks County Almshouse by CHARLES HOFMANN, *1878*

PLATE 99

The Merrimac and Monitor BY R. BARNES, 1891

PLATE 100

Emblem of Sargis Lodge BY CHARLES S. RALEIGH, ABOUT 1885

PLATE 101

NOTES ON THE ARTISTS

The biographical information on these pages is based on data available on twenty-nine of the forty-six known artists, examples of whose works appear in this book. Details on the remaining seventeen have not yet been found. The plate numbers of the illustrated paintings are in red.

BADGER, JOSEPH [1708–1765]

Joseph Badger was born in Charlestown, Masschusetts, in 1708. He was a house painter and glazier who turned his hand to painting portraits. In 1733 or thereabouts he established himself in Boston and painted many portraits of the ladies and gentlemen of that city. He died in Boston in 1765.

12. *Mrs. Isaac Foster*

BRADLEY, JOHN [active 1837–1845]

John Bradley was active as a painter of portraits and miniatures in New York City during the period 1837–1845. The dates of his birth and death are not recorded and nothing more about his life is known. An itinerant portrait painter who signed his work "I. J. H. Bradley" was working in the Hudson Valley at about the same period, and there is some confusion between the two.

72. *Little Girl in Lavender*

BRITTON, WILLIAM [active about 1820]

No biographical information about this painter has come to light except for the fact that he was painting in Germantown, Pennsylvania, about 1820.

44. *Market Square, Germantown, Pennsylvania*

BUNDY, HORACE [1814–1883]

Horace Bundy was born in Hardwick, Vermont, in 1814. He was an itinerant painter of landscapes and portraits in Vermont and New Hampshire. He died in Concord, New Hampshire, in 1883.

67. *Vermont Lawyer*

CHAMBERS, THOMAS [about 1808–died after 1866]

Thomas Chambers was born in England about 1808 and came to the United States in 1832. He was a painter of marine views, landscapes, and portraits. He lived and worked for long periods in New York City, Albany, and Boston. Some of his paintings were "inspired" by engraved views of American scenery; his distinctive manner of painting, however, always gives his pictures a highly individual character. There are no records of his later career, and the place and date of his death are not recorded.

79. *Hudson River Valley, Sunset*
73. *The Constitution and Guerrière*

CHANDLER, WINTHROP [1747–1790]

Winthrop Chandler was born in "Chandler Hill" in Woodstock, Connecticut, in 1747. Most of his life was spent in Woodstock but he did live for several years in Worcester, Massachusetts. It is presumed that he was trained as a house and sign painter by being apprenticed to a house painter in Boston. Most of Chandler's paintings are portraits of his relatives and friends in Woodstock and Worcester, for he never traveled about the country as an itinerant artist. He was never able to earn much money and he died in Woodstock in poverty.

20. *Captain Samuel Chandler*
21. *Mrs. Samuel Chandler*

DE LACLOTTE, HYACINTHE [active 1811–1818]

Hyacinthe De Laclotte was born probably in France. He was active in New Orleans as architect, engraver, scene painter, and drawing teacher from about 1811 to 1815. In 1818 a man named Hethe Laclotte was listed in the Philadelphia Directory as "engraver and architect." Perhaps Hyacinthe and Hethe were the same person. Details of his later career and the date of his death are not recorded.

36. *The Battle of New Orleans*

DURAND, JOHN [active 1766–1782]

John Durand was born probably in France. He first appears as a painter of portraits in 1766 in New York City, where he advertised himself as a teacher of painting and drawing. He painted in Connecticut and Virginia, where he is said to have produced a great number of portraits. He was painting in Virginia as late as 1782, but there is no further record of his career.

16. *Mary Boticon Lathrop*
14. *Sarah Whitehead Hubbard*

EARL, RALPH [1751–1801]

Ralph Earl was born in Worcester County, Massachusetts, in 1751. It is not known where he received his training, but he was probably apprenticed in the usual way to a house and sign painter. Just at the beginning of the Revolutionary War he established himself as a portrait painter in New Haven, Connecticut, but his strong Tory sympathies forced him to flee to England in 1778. He remained in England for about six years, painting portraits in London. He returned to America in 1785 and painted portraits and landscapes in various parts of New England. He died at Bolton, Connecticut, in 1801. Richardson says in his book *Painting in America*, "Ralph Earl may be taken as either the most notable of 'untrained professionals' or the most unskilled of the professional painters . . . six years in England made scarcely any impression upon the archaic severity of his Connecticut style."

31. *Mrs. Noah Smith and Her Children*

EARL, RALPH E. W. [1785–1838]

Ralph E. W. Earl was born in England, the son of Ralph Earl the portrait painter from Connecticut. He must have been brought to America as an infant. He was trained as a portrait painter by his father. The young man went to England in 1809 and stayed there for several years; he also visited France before returning to the United States in 1815. For a time he traveled in the South as an itinerant portrait painter. Through marrying the niece of Mrs. Andrew Jackson in 1818, Earl became a sort of "painter in residence" to the Jackson family, both in the White House while Jackson was President and at Jackson's home, "The Hermitage," near Nashville, Tennessee. In these years Earl painted almost nothing but repetitious portraits of Andrew Jackson. He died at "The Hermitage."

32. *Family Portrait*

FIELD, ERASTUS SALISBURY [1805–1900]

Erastus Salisbury Field was born in Leverett, Massachusetts, in 1805. Although he had the opportunity of working in the New York studio of Samuel F. B. Morse for a few months in the winter of 1824, he was in the main a self-taught artist. He painted portraits and a series of fantastic pictures of Biblical and mythological subjects. After his marriage to the artist Phebe Gilmore in 1831 they lived in Hartford, Connecticut, and in several small towns in Massachusetts. The Fields lived in New York City from 1842 to 1848 but returned to Massachusetts and finally settled there in the town of Sunderland in 1859. Field continued to paint until some time after 1876. He died in Sunderland at ninety-five.

77. *"He Turned Their Waters into Blood"*
49. *Mary Werner Bangs*

HATHAWAY, RUFUS [1770–1822]

Rufus Hathaway was born in Massachusetts—probably at Freetown—in 1770. A portrait painter with a knack for wood carving and joinery, he is said to have made the frames for his paintings. The record shows that he started painting portraits in Taunton, Massachusetts, in 1791. In 1795 he married and settled down to live in Duxbury, where he became the town doctor after studying medicine under Dr. Isaac Winslow of Marshfield. He died in Duxbury in 1822.

27. *Lady with Her Pets (Molly Whales Leonard)*

HESSELIUS, JOHN [1728–1778]

John Hesselius was born probably in Philadelphia, the son of the Swedish immigrant artist Gustavus Hesselius. As the child of a painter he probably played with colors and brushes at an early age. He worked as an itinerant portrait painter, traveling through parts of Pennsylvania, Delaware, Maryland, and Virginia. After his marriage he settled in Annapolis, Maryland, where he spent the rest of his life. One of his principal claims to fame is that he was the first to give instruction in painting to Charles Willson Peale, who later became a famous artist in Philadelphia. Hesselius died in Annapolis in 1778.

10. *Margaret Robins*

HICKS, EDWARD [1780–1849]

Edward Hicks was born in Attleboro (now Langhorne) in Bucks County, Pennsylvania, in 1780. For most of his life his home was in Newtown, Pennsylvania. By trade he was a coach and sign painter. Many of his pictures are of religious subjects; perhaps the most famous of these is his *Peaceable Kingdom*, a favorite subject which he painted many times. Hicks was a famous Quaker preacher and played an active part in Quaker affairs. In later life he wrote a book of memoirs, which gives a detailed account of his religious activities. The memoirs were published shortly after Hicks died. Hicks is one of the best-known and most appealing of all the American primitive painters.

53. *Peaceable Kingdom*
75. *The Cornell Farm*
47. *The Falls of Niagara*

HIDLEY, JOSEPH H. [1830–1872]

Joseph H. Hidley was born in Poestenkill, New York, in 1830 and spent his entire life there. His paintings are principally views of his native town and some of the other villages nearby. He died in Poestenkill in 1872.

92. *Poestenkill, New York*

HOFMANN, CHARLES [active 1872–1878]

The records of Charles Hofmann's life are very scanty. He worked in Pennsylvania in the 1870's and, judging by the style of his picture, he must have been an expert sign painter by trade.

99. *Berks County Almshouse*

JOHNSTON (OR JOHNSON), JOSHUA [active 1796-1824]

Joshua Johnston was a Negro portrait painter who flourished in Baltimore, Maryland, in the years 1796–1824. It is possible that he was instructed by the artist Charles Peale Polk, for their paintings are in many respects very similar. Johnston's name appeared for a number of years in the Baltimore City Directories where he is listed as a limner. He must have been one of the very few Negroes who earned a living as a portrait painter at that time.

34. *Edward and Sarah Rutter*
35. *In the Garden*—attributed

KEMMELMEYER, FREDERICK [active 1788–1805]

Little is known about the life of Frederick Kemmelmeyer except that he was living in Baltimore, Maryland, during the period 1788–1805. He painted portraits and miniatures and is said to have worked as a drawing teacher. The dates and places of his birth and death are unrecorded.

26. *The American Star*
29. *Washington Reviewing the Western Army*
     at Fort Cumberland, Maryland

MARK, GEORGE WASHINGTON [?–1879]

George Washington Mark lived in Greenfield, Connecticut, from 1817 until his death in 1879. He came to Greeenfield from New Hampshire. In addition to being a portrait, fresco, landscape, and historical painter, he was probably a sign painter and he is known to have painted free-hand and stenciled decoration on chairs.

65. *Dismal Swamp*

MOULTHROP, REUBEN [1763–1814]

Reuben Moulthrop was born in East Haven, Connecticut, in 1763. By trade he was a wax modeler and waxworks showman. He traveled with his waxworks show through parts of Massachusetts, New York, and Pennsylvania. His portraits are curiously varied in style, as though he had tried to copy the styles of several other painters. He died in East Haven in 1814.

24. *Job Perit*
25. *Sally Perit*

PARK, LINTON [1826–1906]

Linton Park was born probably in western Pennsylvania in 1826. He painted farm scenes and pictures of logging operations. He died in 1906.

90. *Flax Scutching Bee*

PHILLIPS, AMMI [1788–1865]

Ammi Phillips was born in Berkshire County, Massachusetts. He lived for some time in Rhinebeck, New York, and worked as an itinerant painter of portraits in the towns along the Hudson River and in western Connecticut and Massachusetts. He died in Stockbridge, Massachusetts.

59. *Mrs. Mayer and Daughter*—attributed
38. *Alice Slade*
39. *Joseph Slade*

POWELL, H. M. T. [active about 1855]

H.M.T. Powell worked in California, and his pictorial record of his trip to California over the Santa Fe Trail was discovered and published some years ago.

89. *Studebaker in His Wagon-Tire Shop, Hangtown, California*

PRIOR, WILLIAM MATTHEW [1806–1873]

William Matthew Prior was born in Bath, Maine, in 1806. He painted portraits and landscapes as an itinerant in many parts of New England and as far south as Baltimore. In 1841 he settled in Boston and remained there for the rest of his life. Many of his portraits are painted in a flat, simple style; they were painted quickly and sold for very small sums. For pictures painted in a more highly finished style, he charged higher prices. He aimed at mass production, using factory methods, and was prepared to paint anything a customer might desire. One of his specialties was painting portraits of George Washington on glass. He died in Boston in 1873.

87. *The Burnish Sisters*
82. *The Younger Generation*—attributed

RALEIGH, CHARLES S. [1831–1925]

Charles S. Raleigh was born in Gloucester, England, in 1831. At the age of ten he ran away to sea. He is said to have served in the United States Navy during the Mexican War. He later worked as a merchant seaman until about 1870, when he went to Bourne, Massachusetts. There he married and settled in New Bedford, where he worked as a house painter and decorator. His skill with the brush encouraged him to set up a studio in 1877, devoting his time almost entirely to painting ships and marine subjects. In 1881 he returned to Bourne and spent the remainder of his life there. In his last years defective vision forced him to lay aside his brush. He died in Bourne in 1925, aged ninety-four.

98. *Chilly Observation*
101. *Emblem of Sargis Lodge*

STOCK, JOSEPH WHITING [1815–1855]

Joseph Whiting Stock was born in Springfield, Massachusetts, in 1815. In childhood he was badly crippled in an accident. One of his doctors suggested that he take up painting as a means of earning a living. He is said to have produced more than nine hundred portraits. Stock appears to be one of the few primitive painters who kept a diary that has been preserved. From it one gets a vivid picture of the artist, his joys and tragedies, as well as a complete list of his pictures. One of his doctors constructed a special wheelchair which enabled him to travel, and he visited a number of towns in Massachusetts and Rhode Island painting portraits. Most of his life was spent in Springfield, where he died in 1855.

58. *Baby in Wicker Basket*

THEUS, JEREMIAH [about 1719–1774]

Jeremiah Theus was born probably in Switzerland. He came to America with his parents in a group of German-Swiss colonists about 1735. Some time about 1739 he settled in Charleston, South Carolina, where he opened a drawing school and set himself up as a portrait painter. He was very popular and painted practically every person of importance in Charleston society and the surrounding plantations. It is said that he was known locally as "the court painter." He died in Charleston.

13. *Devout Lady*—attributed

VANDERLYN, PIETER [about 1687–1778]

Pieter Vanderlyn was born in Holland and served in the Dutch navy. He came from Curacao to the Province of New York some time around 1718, staying for a time in Albany and later settling permanently in Kingston. It is believed that he was a house painter, who on occasion tried his hand at portrait painting and painting signboards for taverns. His grandson, the artist John Vanderlyn, claimed that his grandfather painted portraits. No definite record of any of these pictures has been found, but a number of early Hudson Valley primitive portraits have been attributed to him.

9. *Young Lady with a Rose*—attributed

WEST, BENJAMIN [1738–1820]

Benjamin West achieved the most improbable transition; he began his career as a primitive painter in rural Pennsylvania and ended it as Historical Painter to the King of England and President of the Royal Academy. West was born in Springfield, Pennsylvania, near Philadelphia in 1738. His earliest efforts at drawing and painting impressed some gentlemen in Philadelphia, and through their efforts the young artist was able to set out to study in Rome in 1760. After three years in Italy he settled in London. In 1772 he was appointed Historical painter to the King. He held the Presidency of the Royal Academy from 1792 until his death in 1820. Perhaps West's greatest importance stems not so much from his paintings as from his influence upon all the young American artists who came to study painting with him–Matthew Pratt, Charles Willson Peale, Gilbert Stuart, Samuel Morse, Rembrandt Peale, Robert Fulton, Washington Allston, John Trumbull, and John Singleton Copley. In Benjamin West, all these pupils found a conscientious teacher and an unfailingly generous friend.

15. *Sarah Ursula Rose*

CATALOGUE NOTES

CATALOGUE NOTES

All the paintings are oils. The State listed is that in which the painting originated or was found. The material (canvas, wood, etc.) shown is that on which the painting was executed; the dimensions are the overall sizes; height precedes width. The frame is identified as ORIGINAL *when it is the one in which the painting was originally framed; as* CONTEMPORARY *when it is a frame of the same period as that of the painting; as* REPRODUCTION *when it is an authentic copy of a frame of the same period as that of the painting. The frame dimension given is its width. The plate numbers are in red.*

1. *Jonathan Benham*
   BY AN UNKNOWN ARTIST, ABOUT 1710
   New York
   Canvas, 44¾×35⅛ inches
   Reproduction 3-inch black ogee molded
   frame

2. *Gentleman of the Ten Eyck Family*
   BY AN UNKNOWN ARTIST, ABOUT 1710
   New York
   Wood, 28¾×15⅜ inches (sight size)
   Original 1¾-inch black reeded frame

3. *Lady of the Ten Eyck Family*
   BY AN UNKNOWN ARTIST, ABOUT 1710
   New York
   Wood, 28×13¾ inches (sight size)
   Original 1¾-inch black reeded frame

4. *The Annunciation*
   BY AN UNKNOWN ARTIST, ABOUT 1710
   New York
   Wood, 23×33 inches
   Original 3½-inch black concave molded
   frame

5. *"Christ Talketh with a Woman of Samaria"*
   BY AN UNKNOWN ARTIST, ABOUT 1710
   New York
   Canvas, 20⅜×26⅛ inches
   Original 2-inch silver burnished carved frame

6. *Catalynje Post*
   BY AN UNKNOWN ARTIST, ABOUT 1730
   New York
   Canvas, 52½×35⅝ inches
   Original 3½-inch black flattish concave
   molded frame

7. *Susanna Truax*
   BY AN UNKNOWN ARTIST, 1730
   New York
   Canvas, 37⅞×32⅞ inches
   Inscribed in upper left: "Susanna Truax—
   Gebooren den 8 J—1726—
   Geschildird Maart 1730"
   Original 3-inch black flat frame

8. *Lady with Beaded Headdress*
   BY AN UNKNOWN ARTIST, ABOUT 1730
   New York
   Canvas, 23⅝×20 inches
   Original 1-inch brown stippled molded frame
   with black flat outer member

9. *Young Lady with a Rose*
ATTRIBUTED TO PIETER VANDERLYN, 1732
New York
Canvas, 32⅛×27⅜ inches
Inscribed in lower left: "Geschildered 1732"
Contemporary 3½-inch black flat frame with
  wide gold-leaf carved inner member

10. *Margaret Robins*
BY JOHN HESSELIUS, ABOUT 1745
Maryland
Canvas, 26×24 inches
Original 2-inch brownish-black frame with
  carved inner member with traces of
  gold leaf

11. *Young Lady with a Fan*
BY AN UNKNOWN ARTIST, 1737
New York
Canvas, 38×31¾ inches
Inscribed in lower right: "AEtate 19, AD 1737"
Original 3¼-inch dull black molded frame

12. *Mrs. Isaac Foster*
BY JOSEPH BADGER, 1755
Massachusetts
Bed ticking, 36⅛×27¾ inches
Inscribed in lower right: "1755" and on back
  of painting: "Eleanor Foster; Only
  Daughter of William Wyer, Esqr. and
  Eleanor, His Wife; was born July 14th,
  1714."
Original 2¾-inch black half receding molded
  frame with gold-leaf carved inner
  member

13. *Devout Lady*
ATTRIBUTED TO JEREMIAH THEUS, ABOUT
  1750
South Carolina
Canvas, 29¾×24¾ inches
Reproduction 2½-inch black molded frame
  with antique gold carved front member

14. *Sarah Whitehead Hubbard*
BY JOHN DURAND, 1768
Connecticut
Canvas, 33×27⅛ inches
Reproduction 3⅜-inch brown frame with
  concave center and gold-leaf hand
  carved front member; gold-leaf dentil
  block near outer edge

15. *Sarah Ursula Rose*
BY BENJAMIN WEST, 1756
Pennsylvania
Canvas, 29×23⅜ inches
Contemporary 3⅜-inch brownish-black
  bolection molded frame with gold-leaf
  inner cove

16. *Mary Boticon Lathrop*
BY JOHN DURAND, ABOUT 1770
New York
Canvas, 35¾×27½ inches
Reproduction 3⅜-inch black half receding
  frame with gold-leaf carved front
  member

17. *Catharine Hendrickson*
BY AN UNKNOWN ARTIST, 1770
New Jersey
Canvas, 46×38 inches
Reproduction 3½-inch black flattish beveled
  frame

18. *The Domino Girl*
BY AN UNKNOWN ARTIST, ABOUT 1775
New Jersey
Canvas, 23×18½ inches
Reproduction 2½-inch black molded
  receding frame with gold-leaf front cove

19. *Miss Denison*
BY AN UNKNOWN ARTIST, ABOUT 1785
Connecticut
Canvas, 34½×27¼ inches
Original 3¼-inch black frame with gilt
    raised engraved outer member and gilt
    inner member

20. *Captain Samuel Chandler*
BY WINTHROP CHANDLER, ABOUT 1780
Connecticut
Canvas, 55×47½ inches
Reproduction 3½-inch dull black concave
    molded frame with gold-leaf inner cove

21. *Mrs. Samuel Chandler*
BY WINTHROP CHANDLER, ABOUT 1780
Connecticut
Canvas, 55×47½ inches
Reproduction 3½-inch dull black concave
    molded frame with gold-leaf inner cove

22. *The Start of the Hunt*
BY AN UNKNOWN ARTIST, ABOUT 1780
Virginia
Canvas, 34¾×54¾ inches
Original 5¼-inch curly maple flat frame with
    black inner and outer edges

23. *The End of the Hunt*
BY AN UNKNOWN ARTIST, ABOUT 1780
Virginia
Canvas, 34½×53⅞ inches
Original 5¼-inch curly maple flat frame with
    black inner and outer edges

24. *Job Perit*
BY REUBEN MOULTHROP, 1790
Connecticut
Canvas, 36⅛×29¾ inches
Inscribed on back of canvas:
    "Job Perit. AEtat. 38, AD 1790.
    Ruben Molthrop, Pinxit"
Reproduction 3⅜-inch black molded frame
    with gold-leaf inner member

25. *Sally Perit*
BY REUBEN MOULTHROP, 1790
Connecticut
Canvas, 36¼×29¾ inches
Inscribed on back of canvas:
    "Sally Perit. AEtat. 29, AD 1790.
    Ruben Molthrop, Pinxit"
Reproduction 3⅜-inch black molded frame
    with gold-leaf inner member

26. *The American Star*
BY FREDERICK KEMMELMEYER, ABOUT 1795
Maryland
Brown craft paper, 22×18 inches
Inscribed in lower right:
    "F. Kemmelmeyer, Pinx"
Original 1¼-inch black frame with gilt
    inner edge

27. *Lady with Her Pets (Molly Whales Leonard)*
BY RUFUS HATHAWAY, 1790
Massachusetts
Canvas, 34½×32¼ inches
Inscribed in lower right:
    "R. H. Oct. 1790" and
    in lower left: "Canter"
Original 2⅞-inch marbleized bolection
    molded frame

28. *Emma Van Name*
BY AN UNKNOWN ARTIST, ABOUT 1795
New York
Canvas, 29¼×23 inches
Contemporary 2⅝-inch gold-leaf concave
    molded frame with carved calf's tongue
    inner member and with beaded insert
    near outer edge

29. *Washington Reviewing the Western Army at
    Fort Cumberland, Maryland*
BY FREDERICK KEMMELMEYER, ABOUT 1795
Maryland
Canvas, 24×37 inches
Reproduction 3-inch black molded frame
    with oil gilding on inner cove

30. *The Home of George Washington, "The
    Father of His Country"*
BY J. WIESS, 1797
Virginia
Canvas, 16×20½ inches
Inscribed on back of painting: "Painted by
    J. Wiess, Mount Vernon, May 19, 1797."
Contemporary 1⅝-inch gold-leaf concave
    molded frame with dentil black inner
    edge and beaded outer edge

31. *Mrs. Noah Smith and Her Children*
BY RALPH EARL, 1798
Vermont
Canvas, 63¾×85¾ inches
Inscribed in lower left: "Ralph
    Earl pinxit 1798"
Reproduction 4-inch brownish-black half
    receding frame with gold-leaf carved
    inner member

32. *Family Portrait*
BY RALPH E. W. EARL, 1804
Massachusetts
Canvas, 46½×63½ inches
Inscribed in lower right:
    "R. Earl Pinxit 1804"
Reproduction 2¾-inch black molded frame
    with gold-leaf inner cove

33. *The Sargent Family*
BY AN UNKNOWN ARTIST, 1800
Massachusetts
Canvas, 38×50¼ inches
Contemporary 3⅛-inch silver-gilt concave
    molded frame with hand carved front
    member

34. *Edward and Sarah Rutter*
BY JOSHUA JOHNSTON, ABOUT 1805
Maryland
Canvas, 36×32 inches
Original 1⅞-inch gold-leaf deep cove frame

35. *In the Garden*
ATTRIBUTED TO JOSHUA JOHNSTON,
    ABOUT 1805
Maryland
Canvas, 28⅛×20¾ inches
Contemporary 2½-inch gold-leaf beveled
    frame with raised outer edge

36. *The Battle of New Orleans*
BY HYACINTHE DE LACLOTTE, 1815
Louisiana
Canvas, 29¼×36 inches
Reproduction 2½-inch blackish-brown
    concave molded frame with gold-leaf
    front member

37. *A Ceremonial at a Young Ladies' Seminary*
BY AN UNKNOWN ARTIST, ABOUT 1810
Virginia
Canvas, 30×39 inches
Contemporary 2⅜-inch gold-leaf carved
    frame with pearl and bar motif near
    front member and ribbon twist design
    near outer edge

38. *Alice Slade*
BY AMMI PHILLIPS, 1816
New York
Canvas, 40⅛×33 inches
Original 1¾-inch black reeded frame

39. *Joseph Slade*
BY AMMI PHILLIPS, 1816
New York
Canvas, 40⅛×33 inches
Original 1¾-inch black reeded frame

40. *Mr. Tiffen of East Kingston, New Hampshire*
ATTRIBUTED TO A. ELLIS, ABOUT 1820
New Hampshire
Wood, 26×19¼ inches
Original 1¼-inch red grooved and molded
    frame with yellow outer member

41. *Oneida Chieftain Shikellamy*
BY AN UNKNOWN ARTIST, ABOUT 1820
Pennsylvania
Canvas, 45⅛×32 inches
Contemporary 4-inch rosewood veneer frame
    with rounded outer edge and gold leaf
    on front cove

42. *Horizon of the New World*
BY AN UNKNOWN ARTIST, ABOUT 1825
New York
Canvas, 30⅝×65¾ inches
Contemporary 2-inch gold-leaf flat molding
    with half round raised outer member

43. *Bowl of Fruit*
BY AN UNKNOWN ARTIST, ABOUT 1830
Pennsylvania
Canvas, 30¾×39 inches
Contemporary 3-inch gold-leaf ogee frame

44. *Market Square, Germantown, Pennsylvania*
BY WILLIAM BRITTON, ABOUT 1820
Pennsylvania
Canvas, 12¼×19⅞ inches
Contemporary 2-inch gold-leaf beveled
    frame

45. *U. S. Revenue Cutter*
BY H. A. ROATH, ABOUT 1825
Connecticut
Canvas, 15⅝×20¾ inches
Inscribed in lower right: "H. A. Roath" and
    in lower center: "U. S. Revenue Cutter"
Contemporary 2½-inch black veneer frame
    with gold-leaf inner liner

46. *The Plantation*
BY AN UNKNOWN ARTIST, ABOUT 1825
Virginia
Wood, 19¾×29½ inches
Original 2-inch black molded frame with flat
    outer edge

47. *The Falls of Niagara*
BY EDWARD HICKS, 1825
Pennsylvania
Canvas, 32×38 inches
Inscription in gold lettering appears as a
    border:
"With uproar hideous first the Falls appear,
The stunning tumult thundering on the ear
Above, below, where'er the astonished eye
Turns to behold, new opening wonders lie,
This great o'erwhelming work of awful Time
In all its dread magnificence sublime,
Rises on our view amid a crashing roar
That bids us kneel, and Time's great God
    adore."
Original black painted border on canvas,
    with black protective wood edging

48. *General Washington on White Charger (Jack)*
BY AN UNKNOWN ARTIST, ABOUT 1830
New York
Wood, 38⅛×29⅜ inches
Original 2⅞-inch silver-lacquer bolection
    molded frame

49. *Mary Werner Bangs*
BY ERASTUS SALISBURY FIELD, ABOUT 1830
Massachusetts
Canvas, 58⅜×30¼ inches
Contemporary 3-inch gold-leaf flattish ogee
    frame

50. *Mrs. John Harrison and Her Daughter Maria*
BY NATHANIEL MAYHEW, 1823
Massachusetts
Canvas, 30×24⅞ inches
Contemporary 5-inch gold-leaf "Sully" frame

51. *Sea Captain Maxwell B. Chace*
BY AN UNKNOWN ARTIST, ABOUT 1835
New York
Canvas, 29×24¼ inches
Contemporary 3½-inch gold-leaf beveled
    frame with rounded raised outer edge

52. *Yankee Clipper "Cardelia"*
BY AN UNKNOWN ARTIST, ABOUT 1830
New York
Canvas, 26½×44 inches
Original 3½-inch black beveled veneer frame
    with gilt raised wave design on inner
    and outer members

53. *Peaceable Kingdom*
BY EDWARD HICKS, ABOUT 1830
Pennsylvania
Canvas, 30×35⅞ inches
Original 2½-inch black flat frame with
    gold-leaf beveled inner edge

54. *Basket of Fruit with Flowers*
BY AN UNKNOWN ARTIST, ABOUT 1830
New Jersey
Wood, 13¹³⁄₁₆×17¹³⁄₁₆ inches
Original 3-inch mahogany veneer beveled
    frame

55. *The Adoration of the Shepherds and the Magi*
BY AN UNKNOWN ARTIST, ABOUT 1830
Pennsylvania
Copper, 30×38¼ inches
Reproduction 2½-inch maple beveled frame
    with flat outer member

56. *Fruit and Flowers*
BY AN UNKNOWN ARTIST, ABOUT 1835
Maryland
Canvas, 26⅞×41⅝ inches
Original 3-inch silver-gilt ogee frame

57. *The Family at Home*
BY H. KNIGHT, 1836
Connecticut
Canvas, 27½×36 inches
Inscribed in lower right: "H. Knight, 1836"
Reproduction 4¼-inch gold-leaf beveled
    frame with flat outer edge and flat
    raised inner edge

58. *Baby in Wicker Basket*
    BY JOSEPH WHITING STOCK, ABOUT 1840
    Massachusetts
    Canvas, 30½×26 inches
    Contemporary 4-inch gold-leaf beveled
        frame with rounded outer edge

59. *Mrs. Mayer and Daughter*
    ATTRIBUTED TO AMMI PHILLIPS, ABOUT 1835
    Connecticut
    Canvas, 38⅛×34¾ inches
    Original 3⅛-inch gold-leaf frame with black
        raised inner and outer edges

60. *Blue Eyes*
    BY AN UNKNOWN ARTIST, ABOUT 1840
    Maine
    Wood, 18×12¾ inches
    Unframed

61. *Agnes Frazee and Child*
    BY AN UNKNOWN ARTIST, 1834
    New Jersey
    Canvas, 30×26 inches
    Contemporary 3-inch silver-gilt flattish ogee
        frame

62. *On Point*
    BY D. G. STOUTER, ABOUT 1840
    Pennsylvania
    Canvas, 18½×21½ inches
    Inscribed in lower left: "D. G. Stouter, Artist"
    Contemporary 2¼-inch silver-gilt ogee frame

63. *The Cat*
    BY AN UNKNOWN ARTIST, ABOUT 1840
    New York
    Canvas, 16×20 inches
    Contemporary 2¼-inch silver-gilt concave
        molded frame

64. *In Full Stride*
    BY AN UNKNOWN ARTIST, ABOUT 1840
    Pennsylvania
    Canvas, 24³⁄₁₆×34⅛ inches
    Original 4-inch gold-leaf concave molded
        frame

65. *Dismal Swamp*
    BY GEORGE WASHINGTON MARK, 1840
    Connecticut
    Canvas, 38×48 inches
    Inscribed on back of canvas:
        "Dismal Swamp, Va. By
        G. W. Mark, Pinxt, 1840"
    Reproduction 4⅜-inch black flat frame with
        gold-leaf beveled front member and
        gold raised outer member

66. *The Hobby Horse*
    BY AN UNKNOWN ARTIST, ABOUT 1840
    Massachusetts
    Canvas, 40⅝×39⅞ inches
    Original 3½-inch gold-leaf deep concave
        molded frame

67. *Vermont Lawyer*
    BY HORACE BUNDY, 1841
    Vermont
    Canvas, 44×35½ inches
    Inscribed on back of canvas: "H. Bundy, 1841"
    Contemporary 2-inch silver-gilt ogee frame

68. *Portrait of a Man*
    BY AN UNKNOWN ARTIST, ABOUT 1840
    Connecticut
    Canvas, 30×24 inches
    Contemporary 3¼-inch yellow molded frame
        with flat outer member and beveled
        inner edge

69. *Portrait of a Woman*
BY AN UNKNOWN ARTIST, ABOUT 1840
Connecticut
Canvas, 30×34 inches
Contemporary 3¼-inch yellow molded frame
with flat outer member and beveled
inner edge

70. *Tea Time*
BY AN UNKNOWN ARTIST, ABOUT 1840
Connecticut
Canvas, 36×28⅞ inches
Contemporary 3⅛-inch gold-leaf concave
molded frame

71. *Man of Science*
BY M. KRANZ [?], 1839
New York
Canvas, 39×33 inches
Inscribed in lower left: "M. . . anz, Fecit. . 39"
Original 1¾-inch gold-leaf flattish cove
frame

72. *Little Girl in Lavender*
BY JOHN BRADLEY, ABOUT 1840
New York
Canvas, 33⅞×27⅜ inches
Inscribed in lower left:
    "by J. Bradley, 128 Spruce St."
Original 2⅞-inch silver-gilt flattish ogee
frame

73. *The Constitution and Guerrière*
BY THOMAS CHAMBERS, ABOUT 1845
New York
Canvas, 24×34 inches
Inscribed in lower left: "T. Chambers"
Contemporary 3⅜-inch silver-lacquer ogee
frame

74. *Indian Lament*
BY AN UNKNOWN ARTIST, ABOUT 1850
New York
Canvas, 25⅛×30¼ inches
Original 2½-inch silver-gilt ogee frame

75. *The Cornell Farm*
BY EDWARD HICKS, 1848
Pennsylvania
Canvas, 36¾×49 inches
Inscribed at bottom: "An Indian summer
view of the Farm & Stock of JAMES C.
CORNELL of Northampton, Bucks
county Pennsylvania. That took the
Premium in the Agricultural Society:
october the 12, 1848. Painted by E.
Hicks in the 69th year of his age."
Original 5⅛-inch beveled oak veneer frame
with raised outer edge

76. *A City of Fantasy*
BY AN UNKNOWN ARTIST, ABOUT 1850
Massachusetts
Canvas, 28⅝×40⅝ inches
Contemporary 2¾-inch silver-gilt concave
molded frame

77. *"He Turned Their Waters into Blood"*
BY ERASTUS SALISBURY FIELD, ABOUT 1845
Massachusetts
Canvas, 30⅛×40½ inches
Contemporary 4-inch black concave molded
frame with gold-leaf front member

78. *"He That Tilleth His Land Shall Be Satisfied"*
BY AN UNKNOWN ARTIST, ABOUT 1850
Pennsylvania
Wood, 22½×29⅞ inches
Original 2⅜-inch blackish-brown concave
frame with gold-leaf inner member

79. *Hudson River Valley, Sunset*
BY THOMAS CHAMBERS, ABOUT 1850
New York
Canvas, 22×29⅞ inches
Contemporary 3-inch silver-lacquer bolection
        molded frame

80. *Peaceful Village*
BY AN UNKNOWN ARTIST, ABOUT 1850
New York
Canvas, 35½×45 inches
Contemporary 2⅜-inch silver-gilt deep cove
        frame with stenciled stripe design

81. *Stylized Landscape*
BY AN UNKNOWN ARTIST, ABOUT 1850
Connecticut
Canvas, 27¾×41½ inches
Contemporary 4-inch rosewood veneer
        frame with gold-leaf rope design on
        outer edge

82. *The Younger Generation*
ATTRIBUTED TO WILLIAM MATTHEW PRIOR,
        ABOUT 1850
Massachusetts
Canvas, 22×27 inches
Original 2⅝-inch mahogany cross grain
        veneer beveled frame with flat raised
        outer edge and gold-leaf inner liner

83. *By the Cool and Shady Rill*
BY AN UNKNOWN ARTIST, ABOUT 1850
New York
Canvas, 18¼×24 inches
Contemporary 2-inch silver-gilt ogee frame

84. *Reception of General Louis Kossuth at New
        York City, December 24, 1850*
BY E. PERCEL, ABOUT 1850
New York
Canvas, 44×63⅛ inches
Reproduction 3-inch brown molded frame
        with gold-leaf inner member and outer
        edge

85. *The Tow Boat Conqueror*
BY JAMES I. EVANS, 1852
New York
Canvas, 40×50 inches
Inscribed at bottom: "The Tow Boat
        Conqueror—Capt. John Heation
        coming from the Balizo, Oct. 29, 1847,
        painted by J. I. Evans for Capt.
        Heation Nov. 1852."
Reproduction 3⅛-inch mahogany cross grain
        veneer frame with gold-leaf inner liner

86. *Memorial to Nicholas M. S. Catlin*
BY SUSANE WALTERS, 1852
New York
Canvas, 39×28⅞ inches
Original 3-inch red marbleized concave
        molded frame with gold leaf on inner
        and outer edges

87. *The Burnish Sisters*
BY WILLIAM MATTHEW PRIOR, 1854
Massachusetts
Canvas, 35½×40⅛ inches
Inscribed on back of canvas:
"Swenia R. Burnish   Fanny P. Burnish
        Age 3 next July   Age 6
        21st 1854   By W. M. Prior
        W. M. Prior 1854   Mar. 25 1854"
        March 26th
Contemporary 3⅝-inch silver-gilt bolection
        molded frame

88. *The Neigh of an Iron Horse*
    BY A. TAPY, 1859
    West Virginia
    Canvas, 14⅛×18⅛ inches
    Inscribed in lower left: "A Tapy, 1859"
    Contemporary 3¼-inch silver-gilt bolection
        molded frame

89. *Studebaker in His Wagon-Tire Shop,*
        Hangtown, California
    BY H. M. T. POWELL, ABOUT 1855
    California
    Canvas, 23½×32½ inches
    Contemporary 3-inch silver-gilt concave
        molded frame

90. *Flax Scutching Bee*
    BY LINTON PARK, ABOUT 1860
    Pennsylvania
    Bed ticking, 31⅜×50½ inches
    Reproduction 2½-inch bronze metal-leaf
        flattish ogee frame

91. *Bare Knuckles*
    BY GEORGE A. HAYES, ABOUT 1860
    New York
    Cardboard, 11⅞×19⅛ inches
    Inscribed in lower left: "Geo. A. Hayes"
    Original 1½-inch molded walnut frame
        with gilt inner liner

92. *Poestenkill, New York*
    BY JOSEPH H. HIDLEY, ABOUT 1855
    New York
    Wood, 19¾×27⅞ inches
    Contemporary 3-inch brown molded frame
        with black raised center member

93. *Mahantango Valley Farm*
    BY AN UNKNOWN ARTIST, ABOUT 1860
    Pennsylvania
    Window shade, 28×35⅜ inches
    Contemporary 3-inch silver-gilt ogee frame

94. *Fruit of the Seasons*
    BY KOST, ABOUT 1860
    California
    Bed ticking, 16¹¹⁄₁₆×29¼ inches
    Inscribed in lower right: "Kost"
    Contemporary 2½-inch rosewood veneer
        frame with gold-leaf inner liner

95. *Confederate Blockade Runner and Union*
        Man-of-War
    BY F. R. MULLEN, 1861
    New York
    Canvas, 23½×36⅛ inches
    Inscribed in lower left: "F. R. Mullen, 1861"
    Original 2½-inch silver-gilt ogee frame

96. *Custer's Last Fight, June 25, 1876*
    BY W. J. WALLACK, 1876
    Nebraska
    Canvas, 60½×73¾ inches
    Inscribed in lower left: "CUSTER'S LAST
        FIGHT. JUNE 25th, 1876" and
        "W. J. Wallack, Artist"
    Reproduction 4¾-inch rosewood veneer
        beveled frame with flat raised outer
        edge and gold-leaf inner liner

97. *The Circus*
    BY A. LOGAN, 1874
    New York
    Canvas, 24×38 inches
    Inscribed in lower left: "A. Logan, 1874"
    Original 2⅞-inch silver-gilt deep concave
        molded frame

98. *Chilly Observation*
    BY CHARLES S. RALEIGH, 1889
    Massachusetts
    Canvas, 30×44¹⁄₁₆ inches
    Inscribed in lower left: "C. S. Raleigh, 1889"
    Reproduction 3¾-inch rosewood beveled
        frame with gold-leaf inner and outer
        members

99. *Berks County Almshouse*
   BY CHARLES HOFMANN, 1878
   Pennsylvania
   Zinc, 32½×39½ inches
   Inscribed in lower right: "1878—Charles
      Hofmann, Painter" and at bottom
      center: "Views of the Building and
      Surroundings of the Berks-County-
      Alms-House. 1878"
   Original 3-inch walnut deep cove frame
      with gilt inner liner

100. *The Merrimac and Monitor*
   BY R. BARNES, 1891
   Virginia
   Canvas, 36×48 inches
   Inscribed in lower right: "R. Barnes, 1891"
   Reproduction 3½-inch mahogany veneer
      beveled frame

101. *Emblem of Sargis Lodge*
   BY CHARLES S. RALEIGH, ABOUT 1885
   Massachusetts
   Canvas, 44⅜×36⅛ inches
   Inscribed in lower left: "C. S. Raleigh"
      and in gold lettering at top:
      "SARGIS LODGE"
   Original 3-inch red reeded frame with two
      black lines and traces of gold on inner
      member

INDEX OF ARTISTS

INDEX OF ARTISTS

American Primitive Artists

The complete manufacturing of this book has been executed
by Book Craftsmen Associates, Inc., of New York, New York
at the Lakeside Press, R. R. Donnelley & Sons Company,
Chicago, Illinois and Crawfordsville, Indiana. Illustrations of
all the paintings are from Ektachromes by Henry Beville of the
National Gallery of Art, Washington, D.C. The composition,
in Monotype Caslon No. 337, is by Clarke & Way, Inc. The
paper for the text, Bookman Antique Vellum, was especially
made by the S. D. Warren Company of Boston, Massachusetts with art reproductions on Warren
Gloss Coated Enamel. The binding
is in Joanna Natulin cloth.